THE WONDERFUL TOWER OF HUMBERT LAVOIGNET

Lynne Alvarez

BROADWAY PLAY PUBLISHING INC
224 E 62nd St, NY, NY 10065
www.broadwayplaypub.com
info@broadwayplaypub.com

THE WONDERFUL TOWER OF HUMBERT LAVOIGNET
© Copyright 1990 Lynne Alvarez

All rights reserved. This work is fully protected under the copyright laws of the United States of America. No part of this publication may be photocopied, reproduced, stored in a retrieval system, or transmitted, in any form or by any means, electronic, mechanical, recording, or otherwise, without the prior permission of the publisher. Additional copies of this play are available from the publisher.

Written permission is required for live performance of any sort. This includes readings, cuttings, scenes, and excerpts. For amateur and stock performances, please contact Broadway Play Publishing Inc. For all other rights please contact the author's estate c/o B P P I.

First edition: April 1990
This edition: October 2017
I S B N: 978-0-88145-083-5

Book design: Marie Donovan
Word processing: WordMarc Composer Plus
Typographic controls: Xerox Ventury Publisher, Professional Extension
Typeface: Palatino

THE WONDERFUL TOWER OF HUMBERT LAVOIGNET was originally produced by Capital Repertory Company in Albany NY, opening on 12 April 1985 with the following cast and creative contributors:

JOHNNY SNOWALKER .... Maury Cooper
HUMBERT LAVOIGNET .... Barry Snider
CONSTANCE LAVOIGNET .... Phyllis Somerville
ARNOLD TYLER .... Richard Zobel
MICHAEL LAVOIGNET .... Michael Dolan

Director .... Susan Gregg
Scene and lighting design .... Dale F Jordan
Costume design .... Lloyd Waiwaiole

CHARACTERS

In order of appearance:

JOHNNY SNOWALKER, *itinerant Indian fiddler, seventies*

HUMBERT LAVOIGNET, *unemployed postal worker, opinionated, late forties, dreamer of unmanageable dreams*

CONSTANCE LAVOIGNET, *determined, sensual, direct, HUMBERT's wife, early forties*

ARNOLD TYLER, *telephone lineman, mid-thirties, dreamer of manageable dreams*

MICHAEL LAVOIGNET, *teenage son, athletic, high-strung*

The play takes place over a few years in a small Midwest township.

Scene One

(JOHNNY SNOWALKER *walks down a road playing* "The Yellow Rose of Texas" *on his fiddle. We also hear faint thunder.*)

(JOHNNY *is quite old. He is wearing a cotton plaid shirt, a leather vest, Levis, boots. All are very worn. He has on a sweat-stained, wide-brimmed hat covered with metal pins from county fairs, ballparks, circuses, and so on. His fiddle case is strapped to his back and contains his belongings.*)

(*Thunder, lightning. We hear a car approach, headlights.* JOHNNY *tries to hitch. The car whizzes by. Thunder, lightning.*)

(*In a flash of lightning, we see* HUMBERT LAVOIGNET, *sitting on the porch of a small wood frame house. He is staring straight ahead and dressed in an undershirt and boxer shorts.*)

(JOHNNY *catches sight of him.*)

JOHNNY: Well I'll be. (*Approaching*)
You sure spooked me,
But then again, I never did see a ghost in skivvies.
(JOHNNY *sits rigidly.*)
Don't mean to be pushy but it's late, it's goin' to rain, and embarrassin' as it is—I'm lost.
I mean, I been a trapper, a tracker, an escap-ee—Yessir. And you can take my word for it, this is the first time I've been lost. Johnny Snowalker's the name
(*Holds out his hand*)
and I'd be obliged if you would point me to the nearest town—one with a bar in it. This ain't a dry county, is it?

(He waits. Moves his hand before HUMBERT's *unblinking eyes)*
I see you're lost yourself.
Well, sorry to bother you.
(Passes his hand before his face as before)
Maybe you'd like a song. Somethin' to cheer you up.

(He plays "The Tennessee Waltz". HUMBERT *stands up and starts turning around.)*

JOHNNY: I'll be damned. A music lover.

(When JOHNNY *stops playing,* HUMBERT *stops turning.* JOHNNY *plays again.* HUMBERT *turns around and around.* JOHNNY *stops.* HUMBERT *stops.)*

*(*JOHNNY *plays again, just a little bit longer than before.)*

JOHNNY: *(This time, when* JOHNNY *stops,* HUMBERT *continues.)*
Thatta boy.
You should take up an instrument.
(We hear a car approach. Headlights approaching.)
I better get a move on. This'll be my ride.
*(*JOHNNY *holds out his thumb. All of a sudden the car turns on a red light, a siren.* JOHNNY *takes off. Car follows.)*
Aw shit!

*(*CONNIE *comes to the door and turns the porch light on.)*

CONNIE: Honest to God, Humbert, what are you doing out there naked as a fool?!
(She puts on a faded cotton robe and comes out.)
Do you think you're dancing to music?
That's thunder Humbert.
Thunder and lightning.
(She goes out to fetch him.)
All right honey.
Come on now.
Let's get a move on.
(He resists.)

I'm serious.
(He keeps turning, arms outstretched. CONNIE *has to duck.)*
For Christssakes, will you stop turning like a goddamn weather vane.
(He continues. She retreats to the porch.)
All right.
You stay there and freeze to death.
See if I care.
Probably be better if you died anyways,
what good are you like this!
(She watches him.)
Two years, Jesus,
no one else goes to pieces 'cause they lose their job.
I think this is just an excuse to sit around the house.
I do.
It was a crummy job, anyways.
A mailman is not a big deal in the scheme of things Humbert.
Not a speck in the eye of God.
Why you just froze up like this because they replaced you
with a truck, I'll never know. You always complained about your bicycle.
Hell,
I can't stand it.
You look like an idiot.
(She is determined, and goes out to get him again. This time he marches stiffly, with CONNIE *pushing. He gets up the porch.)*

CONNIE: Good. Good.
This is really exciting.
What fun.
Now sit, Humbert—sit!
(She whacks him at the waist so he bends and she can seat him.)
Fine.
(She wipes him off and wraps him in a blanket. It is raining.

We hear it. CONNIE *wipes herself off and lights up a cigar. She stares into the rain. An echo of* JOHNNY's *fiddle.)*
March.
Winter's tail end,
winter's hiney.
And where are we?
You, well, just look at you....
And me?
I'm forty. Halfways to heaven.
(She sighs and smokes.)
You know, you're right, Humbie.
The rain does sound like music.
Like music and I want to dance.
(She watches the rain. Faint thunder. Faint lightning. Sound of rain. We hear a police siren. Lights dim.)

End of Scene One

Scene Two

(It is a Sunday morning in June, bright, sunny. We see the exterior of a modest frame bungalow. HUMBERT *is seated on the porch wearing a cap, and a plaid shirt partially tucked into his jeans. He is barefoot and sits rigidly as before.)*

(Stage right is a small fruit and vegetable stand with a large sign that reads "HOMEMADE BREAD, FRESH DAILY." The stand has melons, cucumbers, beans, etc. A bag full of empty cans lies near the porch.)

(Center stage, CONNIE *and* ARNIE *are finishing a poker game.* CONNIE *is dressed in her Sunday best which includes a small hat.* ARNIE *has on work clothes.)*

ARNIE: *(Happily)* Okay.
(Lays down his hand with a flourish)
Full house!

CONNIE: Royal flush!

ARNIE: Shit!

CONNIE: You owe me 20 dollars!

ARNIE: Well, goddamn, monkey-screwing son-of-a-bitch!

CONNIE: Arnie. You swear too much.

ARNIE: *(Getting his money out)*
I can't help it. My mother always swore.
(MIKE *jogs in, checks his watch, and keeps jogging in place.)*

CONNIE: *(To* MIKE*)* Hi, sweetheart.

ARNIE: Hey there, Mikey.

MIKE: Mike.

CONNIE: Run your ten miles?

MIKE: Almost.

ARNIE: Wish you'd come over here and play a hand or two with us.

MIKE: Runners in my bracket don't sit around playing cards.

ARNIE: We need a man here.

CONNIE: Amen.

ARNIE: I'm serious. I don't feel the right kind of satisfaction if I win
from a woman.

CONNIE: Win!
Cross that bridge when you come to it.
(Car horn honks.)
Mikey, will you get that?
Bread's at one-fifty. Cuke's four for a dollar.

(MIKE *grabs a loaf from the stand and runs offstage.* CONNIE *clears the table.)*

ARNIE: I don't know how you do it all, honey.
You're a miracle worker.

CONNIE: I'm just a worker.
Miracles bring in more than one-fifty a piece.

ARNIE: *(Counting through a wad of bills)*
You know, I'm stringin' these here telephone cables like they was party ribbons. 350 new lines in the next three weeks....
Township's really growing.
I figure civilization's fillin' up my pockets...
so I might as well spread it around a little.

CONNIE: We don't take charity.

ARNIE: Long-term loans?
(CONNIE *shakes her head.* HUMBERT *seems to twist in his seat, groans.*)
You're a hard woman to please.
(She goes and sits next to HUMBERT.*)*
I said, she's a hard woman to please, old buddy.
(He sticks some money in HUMBERT's *pocket.*
To CONNIE:*)*
All right. All right.
We'll stick to Sunday poker.
(MIKE *comes in and hands her some change. He checks his watch and jogs in place.*)

MIKE: I can take care of Dad now.
You can still make the eleven o'clock service.

CONNIE: I suppose so. What time is it?

MIKE: Ten forty-five and forty-three seconds.

CONNIE: Don't give me the seconds. You make me feel rushed.

ARNIE: I'll run you over in my sexy white van.

MIKE: You don't have to. She's got time.

ARNIE: No trouble.

MIKE: I don't think it's necessary....

CONNIE: Stop acting like a pill, Mikey.

MIKE: Mike.

CONNIE: Honestly, I don't know what's gotten into you. I liked you better when you were a swimmer.

ARNIE: Shaved his head—
(Laughing)
Bald as a baby's butt.

CONNIE: Oh my God.
(She is laughing too.)
Everyone thought he had ringworm.

MIKE: Yeh? Well, it worked.
I won two all-state trophies.

CONNIE: *(Laughing)* I know. I know.

MIKE: Mom, quit it!

CONNIE: I'm sorry. It was funny.
(She continues laughing as she enters the house.)

ARNIE: Still workin' off those hormones, eh, old buddy?
(Grabs MIKE playfully)

MIKE: *(Getting free and stopping his watch. He's not jogging.)*
I don't see why you guys still play poker. Must be boring. Just the two of you.

ARNIE: Nope.

MIKE: I bet my mom thinks it's boring.

CONNIE: *(Comes out with her purse and gloves)*
Let's get a move on.
(Kisses MIKE)
Love you, sweetheart.

MIKE: That perfume's awful!

CONNIE: You'll like it better when you're older!
(She pinches his cheek.)
Get all those cans together, hon. Arnie'll cash them in for us.

MIKE: Yes, Ma'am.

CONNIE: 'Bye, Humbert, I'll pray for you.
(HUMBERT *twists in his chair but quiets down right away.*)

ARNIE: See ya, Mikey.
(They exit. We hear the van pull away.)

MIKE: Mike.
Goddamn it.
(Thunder rumbles. HUMBERT *twists in his chair.* MIKE *studies the sky and then watches his father.)*

HUMBERT: Uhhhhh.

MIKE: Yeh, I think so, too.
(Bends close to him)
Dad?
Can you hear me?

HUMBERT *(Agitated, jerky movements)* Uh! Uh!

MIKE: Aw, don't worry, Dad. It won't rain.
It's only thunder. Summer thunder—
Not a cloud in the sky.

(HUMBERT *is quiet.* MIKE *sets his watch and starts jogging in place again near his father. After a while he sits down next to him.)*

MIKE: You know, this really isn't a great time in my life, I don't know why....
I grew two inches this month—that should make me feel good—
guess I'm about as tall as you now—
probably won't grow much more....
School's out—that's okay—not a lot of kids around though,

but runners in my bracket don't have time to hang out anyways.
I'm up to 10 miles a day—they say that's about as much as you should train....
(Pause)
But I don't know, maybe I could push it.
I never trust those experts anyways—
one year they tell you ten miles' the limit, the next year they're swearing twelve is better, or two.
I hear it all the time on the radio,
the final ultimate word,
"Take this drug and save your life."
Six months later they're back with emergency bulletins telling you,
"This drug is a hazard to your health."
I don't know what to think, Dad...things are getting to me....
Even running.
I like to be out there all alone, but then sometimes it gets lonely.
I miss people, you know?
Dad?
(He peers into his face, expectantly. Gets up again, checks his watch, and starts jogging.)
Another two-tenths of a mile.
(Thunder)
What do I know, maybe it will rain, right?

HUMBERT: Sounds like rain.

MIKE: Dad?

HUMBERT: Son, do you have any idea what time it is?

MIKE: Dad?!
Oh, my God!
(He hugs him.)

HUMBERT: *(Laughs)*
Calm down there.

(Patting him)
Hey now, what is it?
What's all the ruckus, boy?

MIKE: Wait 'til Mom hears about this.

HUMBERT: *(Testing his arms and legs)*
Funny, I feel like a bike that's been left out in the rain....
(Makes creaking noises and puts on an old man's voice)
You better give me a hand, Son. I've aged overnight.

MIKE: Overnight?
Are you serious?

HUMBERT: Sure. Why?

MIKE: Dad, you've been sitting there for six months!

HUMBERT: *(Sits back down)*
Holy Jesus! Connie! Connie!

MIKE: Mom's at church.
I'll go get her.

HUMBERT: No, wait. Six months?

MIKE: Yeh.

HUMBERT: No shit.
Six months.
What did I do?

MIKE: Nothing.

HUMBERT: Did I say anything?

MIKE: Not a word.

HUMBERT: Six months.
(Thunder rumbles)

MIKE: *(Hugs him)*
I can't believe you're okay.

HUMBERT: *(Addressing the sky)*
Wouldn't let me up for air, would you, big fella?

You sure as hell drive a hard bargain.
(Thunder again)
Sorry.

MIKE: *(Pulls away)* Who're you talking to?

HUMBERT: God.

MIKE: *(Backs farther away)* Oh no.

HUMBERT: Hey, Mikey. Don't worry.

MIKE: Don't be crazy now. Please.

HUMBERT: I did talk to God, Son.

MIKE: Don't say that.

HUMBERT: All right.
(Long pause)
But I did.
I have a lot to tell you.

MIKE: Just don't.

HUMBERT: Hey there, kiddo, only an act of God could keep me away from you and your mother. You know that, don't you?

MIKE: For a minute I thought you were all better.

HUMBERT: He wants me to do something!
He had a voice like...like a scathing flash of lightning and He let me see...everything!
Lit up the world like a light bulb!
Wonderful. It was wonderful!
God told me to do something wonderful!
(Pause)
You say it was six months?

MIKE: Yeh.

HUMBERT: Six months.
Say, you know what?
(MIKE shakes his head.)

I saw you.
You spend too much time alone, Son.
Running down those roads.

MIKE: Runners in my bracket have to be alone.
Inner concentration.

HUMBERT: I see.

MIKE: I got the urge to go running right now.

HUMBERT: Michael.

MIKE: What?

HUMBERT: I'm not crazy.
I can prove it.
Sort of a cheap trick, though, like pulling a rabbit out of a hat.
(Pause)
Okay.
(Takes a deep breath)
You won three marathons.
(Waits. No effect.)
Not bad for a skinny fifteen-year-old kid.

MIKE: Thanks.

HUMBERT: I saw you run them, Son.

MIKE: Bullshit.

HUMBERT: I was there.

MIKE: You were here!

HUMBERT: Okay,
by your own reckoning I was sitting here like dead wood
for six months, but I'm going to tell you some things no one could possibly know,
unless they were right there with you,
looking out from your very own eyes...now just let me see....

Aha! There was the tri-county high-school marathon
in...in...
what month are we in now?

MIKE: June.

HUMBERT: Right! Then the marathon must have been in
April.
I'll just picture it a minute.
(He closes his eyes and concentrates.)
It was April 19th in Ann Arbor.
You pulled a muscle in your groin, hurt like hell,
but you still qualified in two hours and forty minutes as
I recall.

MIKE: Hey!

HUMBERT: Number 21, right? Blue shorts, grey shirt.
At 21.5 miles you dropped five yards off the front pack,
that muscle again.
You thought you'd lost it for sure and then you did a
mile in...
(Concentrating)
4 minutes 49 seconds and sprinted in first.

MIKE: That's right.

HUMBERT: I was real proud of you, Son.
Hold on a second. There's more....

MIKE: How'd you really know that?!

HUMBERT: Mysterious are the ways of the Lord, eh,
buddy boy?
The next race was in Evanston, Illinois, by special
invitation,
no less...hmmnnn...
and there was this guy you were real worried
about...Roland....

MIKE: Roland Summers!. That's right!

HUMBERT: You'd heard he'd run the course in two hours thirty-five minutes and you just expected to shadow him, jack up the pace a bit, am I correct?

MIKE: Yeh. Absolutely!

HUMBERT: He snapped a tendon.
(Snaps his fingers)
Just like that and you finished the race in two hours forty-two minutes twenty-six seconds...coming in first again!

MIKE: That's amazing!
Fucking amazing!

HUMBERT: Damn straight it is! Amazing?
I mean there I was, no job, no education to speak of. What could a man like me possibly do in the world? But He showed me. He grabbed me by the shoulders and showed me things...unbelievable things...the veins of silver in the ocean, sea creatures buried on the mountaintops, nations asleep with dreams drifting up like swirls of smoke. I saw fingers and eyes and a million hearts beating...I saw beating hearts! God wouldn't let me go.

MIKE: What does He want you to do?

HUMBERT: I don't know.

MIKE: A miracle?

HUMBERT: *(He roams around the yard, picking up things and discarding them.)*
I don't know.

MIKE: Did He give you a hint?

HUMBERT: No.
He took a poor, dejected human being and lifted me up...up....
(Pause. He looks up.)
Well, I'll be damned.

MIKE: What?

HUMBERT: I mean, He took me waayyyy up.
Changed my perspective, so to speak. Made me smaller and bigger at the same time.
(Looks up)
He lifted me up...hmmmmmmmm.
(He goes to the cans and opens the bag.)

MIKE: What're you doing?

HUMBERT: Instead of a little fool with little dreams, He made me into a little fool with big dreams!

MIKE: Yeh?

HUMBERT: Son, I'm going to build the tallest, most beautiful damn tower you ever saw.
A tower so high, it'll take your breath away...and woven...out of things...everything...a filigree tower.
We have the makings right here!
(He pours out the bag of cans and goes through them.)
The silver ones here.
Gold ones here!
Silver ones here!
Gold ones here!
We'll need thousands of these. Scour the neighborhood!

MIKE: The town!

HUMBERT: The entire state!

MIKE: We'll need millions!

HUMBERT: That's a boy!
(They sort through the cans. We hear fiddle music, faintly: "The Yellow Rose of Texas." The lights turn blue.)

MIKE: Jeez, Dad, how did you know it was God?
I mean, did He come right out and say
(Lowering his voice)
HEY, MAN, THIS IS GOD?!
I mean this is amazing.

Fucking amazing.
(Pause)
I didn't even think God worked this way anymore!

(Lights out)

End of Scene Two

Scene Three

(The stage is dark except for a spot on JOHNNY, *far right. He is dressed as before, but we see him through the bars of a jail cell.)*

JOHNNY: I ain't a vagrant.
Vagrants got no folks and no place to go.
I know jest where I'm goin'. Got people there, too, and my people's people.
Yessiree, I got an e-xact destination.
Don't know the precise name, but I got an e-xact picture in my mind.
There's a meadow with yeller grass up to my hip and a stream rollin' through to one side of the foothills of a two-peaked mountain.
Snow line's pretty low.
I like snow.
Johnny Snowalker's the name.
And I ain't no vagrant.
My pa was a red-haired cowboy from Bisbee, Arizona, but my ma was a full-blood Laguna Pueblo.
So I got people.
I got resources too.
You caught me a little short at the moment, but I'm a travelin' fiddler.
What'd y'all like to hear?
The Tennessee Waltz?
The Yeller Rose of Texas?
I play other states, too, Arkansas Traveler, Oklahoma,

Mississippi Mud!
For two bits I'll sing you a chant that'll make your corn grow right past your eyebrows...or what you got around here...deer?...moose?...I got an old Cree song good for moose.
And that ain't all. In case of emergency, lookee here.
Can you see my gold tooth?
Yesiree like money in the bank.
So though I'm very much obliged to ya fer the meals and the roof over my head, you can let me out now. I'm rested and I got to get goin'. Got plenty of ground to cover.
(Waits, paces)
I really got to get a move on. Did you hear me?
(Shakes his head, gets out his fiddle, and tunes as he talks)
I'll tell you what. I'll play ya a little refrain while you're thinkin' it over. One, two, one, two, three, and....
(He sings, sometimes just fiddling, sometimes only singing the words to "Goin' Down this Road Feelin' Bad.")

End of Scene Three

Scene Four

(It is late evening, a week later. Stage right is lit with a blue light. Stars are out. We hear night sounds, crickets, etc. We can barely make out MIKE filling the yard with row after symmetrical row of cans which gleam faintly to gold and silver in the starlight. The rows begin to look like the long, faceless lines of graves in an Army cemetery.)

(Stage left is the darkened interior of CONNIE and HUMBERT's bedroom, now lit by starlight and perhaps porchlight. The room has dark walls and there is a bedside stand, a flower print on the wall. The paint is peeling. HUMBERT is wearing shorts and stands near the window. CONNIE lies in bed in a nightgown.)

CONNIE: Humbert?

HUMBERT: Shhhhhhhh.

CONNIE: He can't hear us.

HUMBERT: I hope not.

CONNIE:...and he can't see us....

HUMBERT: Bet he knows what's going on though.

CONNIE: I hope the whole wide world knows....
(She stretches languorously.)
Mmmmmmm.
Come on back to bed, honey.

HUMBERT: You bet!
(He jumps in bed. They kiss.)
Lord, I wish I was a pervert!

CONNIE: Humbert!

HUMBERT: Well I do.

CONNIE: What are you talking about?

HUMBERT: If I were a pervert, we could do all kinds of things....
Grrr....
(He tickles her.)

CONNIE: You fool.
(They kiss.)
I love you.
(They kiss again.)

HUMBERT: Wait just a minute there!
(He bolts out of bed and runs offstage.)

CONNIE: Honest to God, Humbert, where are you going?!
(She waits. He doesn't answer. She stretches again, gets up, and goes to the window.)

HUMBERT: *(From offstage)*
Get back in bed. Quick!

CONNIE: Okay. Okay.
(CONNIE *gets into bed.* HUMBERT *rushes back in, carrying a beer can on a plate. A flower is stuck through the opening. He presents it to her with a flourish.)*

HUMBERT: You see, I didn't forget
just what you like after a good....

CONNIE: Humbert!

HUMBERT: After a good Humbert!
(HUMBERT *gets into bed. They sit there, sipping beer for a moment.)*

CONNIE: I can barely believe we're lying here together again.

HUMBERT: I know.

CONNIE: I thought I'd lost you forever.
I'm telling you, I can't believe it.
(She tries to hug him. It is awkward because of the beer.)
Put that thing on the floor a minute.
(He does.)
Now hold me.
(He does.)
Tighter, tighter.

HUMBERT: Do you believe it now?

CONNIE: Not yet.
Tighter. Tighter.
There!
(HUMBERT *kisses her.)*
You taste like beer.
But I like it...
and the sheets smell like you.....MMmmmmmm.
I'm going to leave them on this bed 'til they fall apart.
Then I'll be sure you're back for good.

HUMBERT: Of course I'm back for good.
I couldn't stay away from a woman like you.

CONNIE: Well, it happened once.

HUMBERT: You're a good woman, Con.

CONNIE: Not always.

HUMBERT: Always.

CONNIE: There were times....

HUMBERT: Shhhhhhh.

CONNIE: You should know.

HUMBERT: I know.

CONNIE: Humbert....

HUMBERT: I know.
You mean times at the Strathmoor Lounge?
There you were, silver earrings, low-cut dress, soft blue lights,
slow sulky music.
You were dying to dance and a whole lot more.

CONNIE: *(Nervous. Lights a cigar.)* Who told you.

HUMBERT: I just know.

CONNIE: People can't wait to talk, can they?

HUMBERT: It's behind us.

CONNIE: Sure,
just like your "trouble".

HUMBERT: It's all behind us,

CONNIE: I wish I could say I'm sorry.

HUMBERT: I know.

CONNIE: It's been worse for Mikey.
He's quiet.
But he's loyal to you.

Men with the men, you know.
He's trying real hard to be a man—for you.

HUMBERT: Don't smoke....

CONNIE: You should talk to him, Humbie. He wants so much to please you.
He shouldn't drop everything like that, though.
Cans, cans, cans. We can't live off five-cent deposits!

HUMBERT: Put out that cigar, please.

CONNIE: Can't live off my breads and pies either.

HUMBERT: Did you hear me?

CONNIE: The cigars?
Yes, I heard you.

HUMBERT: I don't like to see you smoking a cigar.

CONNIE: Really?
Well, that's just why I started. I figured you'd get pissed off and wake up.

HUMBERT: You can stop now.

CONNIE: Now I like 'em.
(Silence)
Bought them with my own money.
(Pause)
When it's your money again, I might consider stopping.
(Show-blows out a long stream of smoke)

HUMBERT: I see.
(Gets out of bed)

CONNIE: You've been up and around a week now.

HUMBERT: I know.

CONNIE: *(Just about in tears)*
Humbie, I don't want to argue about this. Not now.
But it's spilling out of me. I can't help it.
I've been so worried.

HUMBERT: I know.

CONNIE: Stop saying that.
You don't know.

HUMBERT: *(Looking out the window)*
Just believe in God, honey.

CONNIE: What?

HUMBERT: Trust in the Lord.
Isn't that how they say it?
God? Lord? The almighty?

CONNIE: I don't believe my ears. You telling me to believe in God! That's a
laugh. I'm the one who goes to church and talks to Him every damn week.

HUMBERT: I know.

CONNIE: There you go again. Mister Know-it-all.

HUMBERT: JUST BE-LIEVE IN GOD!

CONNIE: Don't you dare stand there yelling at me about God! You coward, you took the easy way out. Sitting there paralyzed while I slaved myself to death!
God! You can't put everything on God!
Next you'll be telling 'em it was God's will you sat there for six months like a bump on a log. Wouldn't that be convenient!
(HUMBERT *hangs his head.* CONNIE *goes to him and brings him to the bed.)*
Oh, Humbie, it wasn't God who kept you away from us, it was your own fear of facing the present.

HUMBERT: I would never do anything to hurt you and Mikey if I could help it.

CONNIE: I forgive you.
It's only human to want to escape.
And I'll tell you a secret.
Something you don't know, Humbie.

That very evening before you opened your eyes,
I was out riding with your best friend,
and I opened the window wide and let the wind
blast through,
and I turned up that radio loud as I could
and I watched the lights fly by
and I put my foot right on top of Arnie's on the gas
pedal and pressed down until we were going 110 miles
an hour.
And the world sped by and there was music and the
warm body of a man next to me.
Let me tell you, Humbert, I thought I was close to God
too.
But it wasn't God in me. It was only me, not wanting
to face what was back here.

HUMBERT: I'm prepared to face whatever I have to.

CONNIE: Are you going to look for a job tomorrow?

HUMBERT: Connie....

CONNIE: Are you?

HUMBERT: Connie, I love you.

CONNIE: And?

HUMBERT: And I can't make things better.
(He gets up and walks out into the yard.)

CONNIE: Humbert.
You have to.
Humbert.
Do you hear me?
Humbert. Oh, Humbie.
You bastard!
(She starts ripping the sheets off and throws them on the floor.)

HUMBERT: *(Goes to* MIKE *and puts his hand gently on the boy's shoulder)*
Hello, Son.

MIKE: Hey there, Dad.

HUMBERT: What're you doing?

MIKE: I don't know.
I just felt like seeing them all spread out.
Like a design.

HUMBERT: Standing in a row.

MIKE: Yeh.
Kinda like soldiers.
(He salutes HUMBERT.*)*
Right?

HUMBERT: *(Sadly, salutes him back)* Right.
(Lights dim)

End of Scene Four

Scene Five

(It's a cool October day. Downstage in a spot is HUMBERT *in fall work clothes hauling a large, unwieldy sack of bottles and cans. He is awkwardly carrying some window screens under his other arm.)*

*(*JOHNNY SNOWALKER *enters and heads right over.)*

JOHNNY: Howdy there, Mister. Need some help?

HUMBERT: Think you can handle it?

JOHNNY: Ain't as puny as I look.
Johnny Snowalker's the name.

HUMBERT: Guess I could use a hand.
Thanks. It's only a few steps.

JOHNNY: *(Taking the sack. It's heavier than he thought.)*
You must be the fellas building the tower.

HUMBERT: What makes you think that?

JOHNNY: Fellas over to the bar was arguin' 'bout you haulin' garbage on foot.

HUMBERT: Garbage, eh?

JOHNNY: Ain't too many folks on foot around here. Mostly cars zoomin' by.

HUMBERT: Arguin'...eh?

JOHNNY: Some said you was makin' art. Some said it was a pile of junk and a public nuisance. Figured I'd like to see for myself. So I been lookin' fer you.

HUMBERT: Well, I'm the one you're looking for, for all that's worth.
Humbert Lavoignet's the name.

JOHNNY: Like to climb the tower.

HUMBERT: It's hardly built yet.

JOHNNY: How high you plannin' to go?

HUMBERT: That's a good question.
(They arrive at the yard. Lights up. We see one huge foot of the base of the tower, taller than the house, rising out of sight. It is made of cable, window frames, bottles, and cans. The stand has pumpkins, squash, apples. In addition to the bread sign is a smaller sign that reads, "HOMEMADE PIES.")

HUMBERT: Well...here we are....
(Sardonically)
That's my wife's thriving business over there
and this is my wonderful tower.

JOHNNY: *(Goes over to it)*
Beautiful piece of work.

HUMBERT: How about a slice of pie and some coffee?

JOHNNY: Much obliged.
Sure would like to climb the tower.

HUMBERT: Help yourself.
(He goes in for some pie.)

(JOHNNY makes his way up the tower.)

HUMBERT: *(Comes out with the food)*
How're you doing up there?

JOHNNY: Can't see far enough yet.
(Comes down)

HUMBERT: What're you looking for?

JOHNNY: Some of my people.

HUMBERT: I know the area fairly well.
So if you tell me where they're staying....

JOHNNY: Don't reckon I know its name now.
But I can describe it to you.
(Pause)
There was a meadow, violets mixed with the grass.
When I saw 'em, children was playin' tag. The men was
fishin' 'n drinkin' beer by a little runnin' stream that
come down from the mountain. A two-peaked
mountain. The wimin' was makin' fires and gossiping.
I could see it so clear. I was climbing up to the
snowline. Always loved the snow, seemed like magic to
me, 'cause I was born on the desert. I was so high I
could see my friend lyin' with a pretty little woman in
the tallest part of the grass, yesiree.
I can still picture it in my mind, clear as can be.

HUMBERT: When were you there?

JOHNNY: 'Bout fifty years ago.

HUMBERT: I see.
(Pause)
And you think they're still at this place?

JOHNNY: Not this place e-xactly. Place like it though.
That two-peaked mountain'd be easy to spot.

HUMBERT: There's no mountains for at least two hundred miles.

JOHNNY: If the tower was high enough now....

HUMBERT: Maybe you wouldn't recognize your people. The children would be all grown and your friend with the woman would be an old man by now.

JOHNNY: Oh, no.
They'd be e-xactly the same.
See, I saw it all so clear, way up there by the snowline.
I saw those ranchers pull up with their trucks.
I saw 'em pour kerosene on the grass and light it with torches.
Didn't take to Indian people camping there, see.
A wall of fire flew up and my people burned and the men were gunned down in the stream.
So I know they never got old. They're the same. Only I got old.
I'm alone now, so I been lookin' fer them.

HUMBERT: But, old man, they died.

JOHNNY: Oh, no.
I don't believe in death.
Live things always spring back. Just in a better place.
Each according to its nature.
If they lived in woods, it's woods.
If they lived on the plains, it's grass rollin' forever under their feet.
(Pause)
Tell you what. Winter's comin'.
I'll stay 'n help you build that tower high as you like.
By spring maybe I could see clear to the Pacific Ocean.

HUMBERT: I'd really like to do that for you, but we're barely scratching through here ourselves.

(Car horn honks.)

JOHNNY: I'm a hard worker, if that's what you mean.

(Car honks impatiently.)

CONNIE: *(Comes onto the porch)*
Aren't you going to get that! Bread's one-fifty and pie's sixty cents a slice.
That'll be sixty cents for you too, Mister.

JOHNNY: *(Jumps up)*
I'll git that, Missus.
(He goes offstage.)

CONNIE: Humbert?

HUMBERT: It's all right, Con.
(Pause)
His name's Johnny Snowalker. Tells quite a tall tale.

(JOHNNY runs back onstage without saying a word and strikes a blatantly corny pose next to the tower. He runs offstage again.)

CONNIE: Birds of a feather!

JOHNNY: *(Reappearing)*
Got two-fifty fer the bread and sold a whole pie.
Got one-fifty fer the photo, too.
So here's your sixty cents, plus some extra.

CONNIE: I can't believe my eyes.

JOHNNY: Hope you don't got nothin' against Indians, Missus. 'Cause I was tellin' your husband here I'm hard up fer a wintering place.

CONNIE: It's awfully small here, Mr. Snowalker.

JOHNNY: I'm clean 'n I get up early. Hardly eat a thing. You can see I'll earn my keep and put money in your pocket.
(Pause)

Tell you what. If I don't work out, you can kick me out in the middle of a snowstorm.

CONNIE: *(Laughs)*
I like the way you talk.

JOHNNY: You bet.
I'm a real entertainer. I've fiddled for every kind of person, junkie to gentleman.

HUMBERT: He'd help with the tower.

CONNIE: Don't talk to me about that damned tower!

HUMBERT: I'll finish it faster, Con.

CONNIE: *(Pause)* Guess you have a deal, Mr. Snowalker. Mr. Snowalker can share the living room with you, Humbert,
so you won't have to sleep alone anymore.

JOHNNY: Much obliged.

CONNIE: *(Starts in and then comes out again)*
Can you play dance music, Mr. Snowalker?

JOHNNY: Sure can.

CONNIE: How about hymns?

JOHNNY: Got just the one!

CONNIE: Why don't you come play your fiddle back by the kitchen for a while.
I sure could use the company.

(They walk around back. We hear JOHNNY *tuning. He begins "Amazing Grace" and goes to "Will the Circle Be Unbroken." We hear it faintly.* HUMBERT *climbs the tower.)*

HUMBERT: Quite a view.
Township's growing. People are spreading over the hills like molasses.
There's ole Arnie stringing up a pole. Working like a son-of-a-bitch. Hey there, Arnie! Over here, old buddy!

(Waits)
Guess not.
(Turns)
Look at that stretch of maple. Sugar maple, black maple, silver maple, red maple, mountain maple, maple paradise....
Uh...there's the highway crew struttin' around....
Think they're hot shit....
Hey, isn't that Mikey smoking near the trailer?!
Michael! Son! Up here! Heyy! Smoking'll slow you down!
Hey there. Look up!
(Pause)
He'll look up. They all will. You just wait. This tower will stop people dead in their tracks. Pink in the morning and orange in the evening. When the sun hits this tower, it'll look like a pillar of fire.

(Lights out)

End of Scene Five

Scene Six

(It is midwinter and CONNIE *and* ARNIE *are driving along in the van.* ARNIE *has on a plaid lumberjack's jacket.* CONNIE *is loosening her winter outer clothing. Perhaps a screen projection behind gives the impression of driving through a winter forest.)*

CONNIE: I'm halfway to heaven, Arnie.

ARNIE: *(Pats her leg)*
Thanks, darling. I like to be with you too.

CONNIE: Halfway to heaven means I'm forty, Arnie.

ARNIE: Oh.

CONNIE: It means one foot in the grave!

ARNIE: It ain't that bad.

CONNIE: Oh, yeh?
How old are you?

ARNIE: How old do I look?

CONNIE: Thirty-eight, thirty-nine, maybe.

ARNIE: Thanks a lot.
I'm thirty-six.

CONNIE: There! You see, forty's old!

ARNIE: Not on you.

CONNIE: You better pull over,

ARNIE: You ain't mad, are you?

CONNIE: Find a nice, quiet spot. I want to talk to you.

ARNIE: We're talking.

CONNIE: I want to be still...and talking.

ARNIE: Sure thing.
(He continues driving.)

CONNIE: Well, not next year.

ARNIE: Hold your horses.
I don't want Humbert peering down at us from his goddamned tower and gettin' the wrong idea.
(He pulls over.)
There. You see.
Open the window a little so you can breathe some fresh air. *(They sit in silence.* ARNIE *whistles to himself.)*
Well, not next year, honey. What do you got on your mind?

CONNIE: I don't know where to begin.

ARNIE: I do.
(He pulls her toward him and kisses her.)

CONNIE: Arnie!

ARNIE: Shit!

CONNIE: *(Laughs)*
What're you swearing for?

ARNIE: I surprised myself.
I've been thinking about doing that for so long.
I'm sorry.
I'm sorry.
(He looks around guiltily.)
I don't know what got into me.
I apologize.

CONNIE: Fine.

ARNIE: You looked so soft and sad there.
Really, I'm sorry.
(He kisses her again.)
I can't help it.

CONNIE: Have you lost your mind?

ARNIE: Yep.
(Pause)
Hey, wait.
Why aren't you fighting me?

CONNIE: Why should I?

ARNIE: What about Humbert?

CONNIE: It's got nothing to do with him. This is between you and me.

ARNIE: Hey. That ain't right. You're married.

CONNIE: You fool.
You were the one who kissed me.

ARNIE: But you know my reputation.

CONNIE: Yes. I do.

ARNIE: Well?

CONNIE: You're perfect.
(Silence)
What's wrong?

ARNIE: *(Suspicious)*
No woman ever called me perfect before.

CONNIE: You are for me. Perfect. A light-hearted lover, nothing heavy, nothing serious.

ARNIE: Just a beam of light in the darkness.

CONNIE: So what do you think?

ARNIE: Well, shit, I dunno.
(Pause)
Do you like me?

CONNIE: Honestly, Arnie.
Of course I like you.
I like your shiny hair, I like your big old hands.
(She kisses him.)
And I like your warm, warm heart.
(They kiss.)
Well?

ARNIE: Just so you keep in mind how I am with women.

CONNIE: Right.

ARNIE: Can't settle down.

CONNIE: That's a good thing.

ARNIE: I really like you, Connie.
I think you're real pretty.
Sexy too.

CONNIE: You too.

ARNIE: And you can forget about this halfway to heaven bit, darlin'.
'Cause we're talkin' all the way.
(He laughs. They kiss.)
But about Humbert....

CONNIE: Let's get this straight once and for all, Arnold Taylor, I don't want to leave Humbert.
I just want to love you.

End of Scene Six

Scene Seven

(It is a late morning in May. JOHNNY is taking down the "HOMEMADE BREAD" sign. He props it against the porch. Then he nails up a sign that reads "TOWER PHOTOS $2.50.")

(HUMBERT stands in the yard, ripping a dress of CONNIE's into long strips. MIKE enters with a window frame.)

HUMBERT: Arnie Taylor for Christsakes!

MIKE: Hey, Dad. What're you doing?!
That's Mom's!

HUMBERT: So what.
She didn't want it. She left it behind.
She left behind everything she didn't want,
didn't she?!
(MIKE is silent.)
No use letting it go to waste.
(He wraps a strip around his hand and flexes it.)
Helps my grip. It's like grabbing hot pokers up there.
We'll have to start working late again.
(MIKE takes the cloth and holds it for a moment and gives it back.)
You could have gone with her.
But you didn't, Son.
Man with the men, right?

MIKE: Right.
(Car horn honks. JOHNNY runs out.)
Maybe you could've explained things to her.

HUMBERT: And have her take me for a madman?!

MIKE: She took you for a fool!

HUMBERT: Watch your mouth, young man.

JOHNNY: *(Returns)*
We got pickled watermelon rind?

HUMBERT: I think we're out?
Mikey?
(MIKE *shrugs.*)

JOHNNY: *(Grabs some jars from the stand and rushes out)*
That's okay!

HUMBERT: Look. Things happen for a reason.
It's painful, but we had to learn the difference
between a church-going and a God-fearing woman!
Where did church-going get her anyways?
For a ride in Arnie Taylor's van, that's where!
Arnie Taylor for Christsakes!
Jesus!
(He grabs the rags and goes up the tower.)

JOHNNY: *(Re-enters)*
Wanted green tomatoes, but I sold 'em three
jars of strawberry jam fer four-fifty!

MIKE: Great.

JOHNNY: We're scrapin' by with grace 'n promise.

MIKE: Grace and promise isn't enough.
I want money.

JOHNNY: We'll be okay.

MIKE: I don't think so.
(Pause)
Hey, Johnny?

JOHNNY: Yep.

MIKE: I've been thinking of digging ditches.

JOHNNY: Fine occupation.

MIKE: The guys said I could lay blacktop too....
I'd make enough money to live on.

JOHNNY: So you're thinking of leaving?

MIKE: I'm almost sixteen....
It'd be a good thing.

JOHNNY: Hard to tell what's a good thing.

MIKE: You don't seem to have much trouble.
You found the tower and figured that was a good thing....

JOHNNY: Maybe so. Maybe not.
Can't judge the end from its beginning.
You just got to wait around and see.

MIKE: Don't give me one of those Indian answers.

JOHNNY: I ain't dodgin', if that's what you mean.
I have learned that from personal experience, Sonny.
Take a tornado for instance.

MIKE: Oh, come on.

JOHNNY: No, listen now, would you say that's a bad thing? Yes or no?

MIKE: Never seen one.

JOHNNY: I seen a lot. Looks plenty bad up close.
The air goes green, then black.
Makes a grindin' noise like a freight train passin' overhead. It'll flatten
your refrigerator and wrap it around a tree; lift
a man from his living room chair, break every bone
in his body and set him down again...now that's pretty bad, ain't it?

MIKE: Yeh, I guess so.

JOHNNY: But then again....
A tornado brought my uncle a pony once...all saddled
up and everything, a real pretty little thing. Landed

right in the front yard. He rode it around for two years; set up a little pony ride for kids; did well; bought his wife a hair dryer and added on to the house. That little pony brought him nothin' but luck. So now, would you still say that tornado was a bad thing?

MIKE: Not for him.

JOHNNY: Maybe. Maybe not. 'Cause later some rich man pulled up in his Chevrolet and called that little pony by its rightful name. It sped right out from under my uncle; broke two of his vertebrae, lost his business, and ended up spending five years in a wheelchair.

MIKE: Oh, God.

JOHNNY: See what I mean?
You got to wait around.

MIKE: No way!
Look what happens if you wait around!
Disaster!
You got to take things into your own hands.
Nature's too unpredictable.

JOHNNY: What is there besides nature?

MIKE: Man.

JOHNNY: Man's different than nature, eh?

MIKE: Yeh, man can take things into his own hands.
He can build something good and it's good and it makes him happy and he can add on to it piece by piece.
And each piece he adds gets better and better...
unless he fucks up.
Take this, for example.
(He indicates the tower.)
The higher we go, the darker it gets.

(HUMBERT *jumps down from the tower, agitated.*)

HUMBERT: Johnny, step over here a minute, will you?
Now take a good look.

(He indicates a place on the tower. They stare at it for a moment.)

JOHNNY: I don't see nothin' much.

HUMBERT: Does that tower look shorter to you?

MIKE: Shorter?

HUMBERT: Yes, shorter!
Where's the tape!
(JOHNNY hands it to him. HUMBERT goes up the tower.)
Maybe I am a stark-raving, senile, paranoid,
hallucinating maniac, but goddamn it, Johnny,
I could have sworn we added three feet to that center section yesterday!

JOHNNY: I reckoned we did too.
Maybe we should write down jest how high we built,
so it won't trouble us.

(HUMBERT comes down again.)

HUMBERT: It's shorter and the top bolts are wobbling
around like an old man's tooth.
The wind wouldn't have done that.

JOHNNY: No wind last night.

MIKE: Neighborhood kids.

HUMBERT: Why would they do a thing like that?

JOHNNY: Pranks maybe.

MIKE: Johnny, do you got a wrench?

HUMBERT: Well, that does it.

JOHNNY: Sure thing.
(Gives it to him)

HUMBERT: We'll work nights.
Right, Mikey?

MIKE: Right.
(Starts up)

HUMBERT: It's awful hot up there.
You want these?
(Starts to unwrap rags)

MIKE: No.

HUMBERT: *(Watching him, to JOHNNY)*
Will you look at him. Physical. That boy is physical.
(To MIKE)
We'll work nights like we did last summer.
That was fun, wasn't it?
(MIKE is silent.)
We had a good time.
It was like a party.
Wasn't it like a party, Mike?
The stars sparkling overhead, trucks and vans
and cars pulling up.
Just like a drive-in movie.
They'd have a beer, watch, make out.
(He laughs, but it turns sad.)
I really liked that.
Connie'd make pies and cakes.
We'd turn on the radio.
The pies and cakes and music and Connie.
Just like a party,
wasn't it, Johnny?

JOHNNY: Yessiree.

HUMBERT: Goddamn party.
(Angrily removes the rags, almost in tears)
I need a break.
Johnny, let's go.
Mikey!

JOHNNY: We could hit them two bars down the road.
They got plenty of bottles and cans and I know for a
fact they'd give us a beer or two fer a coupla my songs.

HUMBERT: Get your fiddle and let's get a move on. You coming, Mikey?

(JOHNNY *gets his fiddle and begins to tune it.*)

MIKE: I'll just tighten these bolts.

HUMBERT: Don't get yourself a sunstroke.

MIKE: You guys go ahead.
You need it.

HUMBERT: We do indeed.

JOHNNY: Ready?

HUMBERT: Yep.
(JOHNNY *starts off.* HUMBERT *hesitates.*)
Mike!

MIKE: Yeh?

HUMBERT: I'll bring something back for you.

MIKE: That's okay.

HUMBERT: I'd like to.

MIKE: Do what you like.

HUMBERT: *(Can't bring himself to leave)*
Yeh. Okay.
Take it easy.

MIKE: I will.

HUMBERT: Keep an eye out.

MIKE: Goodbye, Dad.

(HUMBERT *leaves. Everything is quiet. Perhaps we hear birds or traffic far away, that's how still it is. Then we hear loud banging and wrenching. Pieces of the tower shower down.*)

(HUMBERT *re-enters, guiltily.*)

HUMBERT: Hey, Mikey, I can't leave you up there alone.
(*A big chunk of the tower falls, just missing him.*
HUMBERT *falls back.*)
Hey!

(MIKE *scrambles down the tower and runs to him. He helps his father up.*)

MIKE: Dad? Dad?
Are you all right?
You okay?

HUMBERT: (*Dusts himself off, shaken*)
I told you those bolts were loose!

MIKE: I'm sorry.

HUMBERT: Goddamn it! Look at the mess!
(*They both look around. Pause.*)
Hey, wait.
You weren't tightening those bolts, were you?

(MIKE *looks him dead in the eye but doesn't respond.*)

HUMBERT: Tell me you were tightening those bolts.
Please....
(*Grabs him*)
Go ahead. Tell me!
In the name of God!

MIKE: (*Takes his hands away*)
No.
I wasn't tightening the bolts.

HUMBERT: What do you mean?!

MIKE: I wasn't tightening the bolts....
I was loosening them.

HUMBERT: Michael.
Son...why?

MIKE: It's junk, Dad. It's garbage.
You've been burying us in a pile of junk, a garbage

heap.
The work of God!
How could this be the work of God?

HUMBERT: Hey, now, just a minute.
You believe me, you do, don't you, kiddo?!

MIKE: Nobody believes you.
Nobody cares.
People see me coming and won't open the door.
I work my butt off for you
I make a fool of myself day after day.
They laugh in my face
and the kids....
Forget it!

HUMBERT: Just wait, Mikey.
It'll happen.
Give me a few more days, another month!

MIKE: Another day, another month, another year, who cares?!
In fifty years, a hundred people'll be zooming around in rocketships looking at the stars, and this?
After all we've been through, this'll be gone, forgotten, buried under a forty-lane highway!
And you'll be dead and me and Mom'll be dead and what will it all matter, Dad?
Let's go and get Mom. Please.
Let's bring her back and start over.

HUMBERT: I can't.

MIKE: Yes, you can!
Dad?!
(Pause)
What do you think you're doing anyways?
You're just junking up the landscape.
If you want people to see God so bad why
don't you go plant a tree and have 'em file by to watch it grow?!

HUMBERT: Because one tree isn't enough!
It's the forest they have to see
before the Earth gets poorer and uglier
and the wild animals disappear, and the sky's
poisoned and the land stripped bare
they have to see a hundred miles of trees!
You think I'm a fool and a dreamer like your mother does,
but I'm a realist!
Mikey,
we can't grab people by the scruff of the neck and make
them stoop to see a tree—they'd just argue about the
best bug spray....
But we can lift them up to see a whole forest!
We can!
And what's more, if we have to, we can do it with what
people don't want anymore—with what they leave
behind.
We'll take it all, Mikey,
and we'll use it!

(JOHNNY *re-enters and scans the fallen pieces of tower.*)

MIKE: We is one too many, Dad.

(MIKE *gathers some things to go.*)

HUMBERT: What're you doing?
(MIKE *leaves.*)
Hey! Wait a minute!
(*To* JOHNNY)
Where is he going?!
(*Starts after him*)
Michael!
Wait!

End of Scene Seven

Scene Eight

(It's an evening in July. Thunder. Lightning. The yard is empty of all debris. Everything has been used up. We see the house, the porch. HUMBERT *sits glumly in his boxer shorts and undershirt.* JOHNNY *stands nearby, watching the sky.)*

JOHNNY: Storm'll be here in...oh I'd say about eight and a half minutes.

HUMBERT: Please.

JOHNNY: When the storm leaves, maybe I should foller it.

HUMBERT: You mean leave?

JOHNNY: Can't see there's much for me to do.
We're bogged down.

HUMBERT: It's a pause.

JOHNNY: A pause then.
Still can't see much for me to do.
Everything's used up,
everyone's given up.

HUMBERT: It's a goddamn pause,
I'll get it back.
I always get it back.

JOHNNY: I can't pause.

HUMBERT: Now why can't you pause?

JOHNNY: I'll drop dead.

HUMBERT: I feel like a goddamn straight man here. Why will you drop dead?

JOHNNY: I'm old. Old people die.
A chill, a dampness, the slightest breeze—why, anything

can carry you off when you're old.
Especially waiting.

HUMBERT: I'll go with you.

JOHNNY: Fine company.
Not only don't you know where you're goin', you don't hardly know what you're doin'.

HUMBERT: God wouldn't have given me something impossible, would He?

JOHNNY: It's your vision, Sonny.

HUMBERT: The eternal optimist.
The eternal optometrist.
I need my vision checked.
(Thunder and lightning)
I looked for a sign, all right.
What'd I get?
Bottles and cans.
Lighting flashed. Thunder rolled.
They looked like gold and diamonds to me.
That was my sign.

JOHNNY: Great Medicine is full of signs.
The whole world speaks to you if it's truly great medicine.

HUMBERT: Is that so?

JOHNNY: Look for a sign.

(HUMBERT *stumbles around the yard. He picks up a strip of metal. Shakes his head, drops it, picks up some newspaper.*)

HUMBERT: Nawwww....
(Picks up a stick)
Is this a sign?

JOHNNY: If it's a sign you know it.

HUMBERT: So what the fuck's your sign?
Do you have one?

JOHNNY: Yep.

HUMBERT: Wordy old coot, aren't you?
Well, what is it?

(Lightning flashes. A roll of thunder.)

JOHNNY: You. *(Gets up and dances)*
Hey-ya-ah-na-ah! Hey-ya-ah-na-ah!
Ku-ru-tsu-eh-ah-eh-na! Kuru-tsu-eh-ah-eh-na!
To the east below,
to the south below,
the winter people come.

HUMBERT: There's nothing left! NOT A WIRE, NOT A CAN. NOT A WINDOW FRAME!

JOHNNY: Hey-ya-ah-na-ah! Hey-ya-ah-na-ah!
Ku-ru-tsu-eh-ah-eh-na! Kuru-tsu-eh-ah-eh-na!
To the west below,
to the north below,
the winter people come.

HUMBERT: What are you doing?

JOHNNY: I'm helping.
All medicine is connected.

HUMBERT: Maybe you can conjure Connie back then.
Tell her the yard's all cleaned up.
She'd like that.
Nothing left but the house!
(Thunder and lightning. Thunder. HUMBERT shades his eyes and looks up.)
Aw, shut up!

JOHNNY: *(Goes in the house)*
Porch door's comin' off.

HUMBERT: Well, I'll be.
(Rushes to the porch and takes the screen door off)
Hey, Johnny. Come here!

JOHNNY: Want some coffee?

HUMBERT: Hey there, buddy.
We still have the house.

JOHNNY: I see what you mean.

HUMBERT: Do you?
Do you?
There's window frames and aluminum siding.
There's all that wiring too.
A gold mine!
(He drags the door toward the tower.)

(Thunder and lightning)

JOHNNY: Watch out for the lightning!

HUMBERT: Go ahead. Hit me.
If I'm wrong, strike me dead
right now!

(Thunder and lightning)

End of Scene Eight

Scene Nine

(Two areas of the stage are used. Downstage, MIKE is digging, wearing a T-shirt and jeans. He is listening to a baseball game on the radio.)

(In the second area, we see HUMBERT high in the tower. JOHNNY is at the base, his ear close to the radio, trying to pick up a tune on his fiddle. We can't yet hear what is on the radio.)

(ARNIE walks over to MIKE. MIKE is digging and doesn't notice him. ARNIE turns off the radio.)

ARNIE: How ya doin', Son?

MIKE: Turn that radio on!

ARNIE: Tigers losin' anyways....
(Looks around him)
So, have a fight with the guys?
(MIKE *keeps on with his work.*)

MIKE: I like being alone.

ARNIE: Oh, yeh, that's right. I forgot.
I thought maybe they were picking on you....
We saw those articles about your dad in the paper last week.

MIKE: He's a freak.

ARNIE: Your mom and I kinda thought they made him into a celebrity.

MIKE: If you consider freaks in a sideshow celebrities. Him and Johnny posing and grinning with the house all torn apart.

ARNIE: Funny how those things go.
All those people who pushed him down, now that he's down, can't do enough for him; leaving bags of bottles and scrap metal. Even donated butane and a blow torch. Show me the man who doesn't love an underdog....

MIKE: I don't

ARNIE: So...uh...you like living with those bozos?
(MIKE *doesn't respond.*)
Starting to look like them...not bad.
Turning into a real hunk.
All muscle from the neck down.
You're really growing up.
Seems like I ain't the only one who's noticed.
Certain girl came by and told your mom you've been acting pretty grown up with her.

MIKE: Yeh. So.

ARNIE: The girl's pretty unhappy about it.

MIKE: I didn't do anything to her she didn't want done.

ARNIE: Don't think that's acceptable, Mikey.
(MIKE *doesn't answer.*)
Your mom wants to talk to you.

MIKE: She knows where I live.

ARNIE: She loves you.
You're on her mind a lot.

MIKE: That's her problem.

ARNIE: Gentleman all the way down the line, ain't you....
Well, sorry, that ain't acceptable neither...Mi-key.

MIKE: Mike.

ARNIE: You're actin' like a spoiled brat...Mikey.

MIKE: *(Threatens him with his shovel)*
Get outta here.

ARNIE: Mucho macho, eh.

MIKE: Look. I don't care what's acceptable to you.
Screwin' my mom when she's married is acceptable to you!
Breaking up my family is acceptable to you!
Well, fuck you. Fuck all of you.

ARNIE: I'll say this for you.
You got good comebacks. Fast.
You think fast. Run fast. Fast with the girls.
(Slowly)
You're faster than me, that's for damn sure.
You're like your mom.
(Pause)
That scares me.

MIKE: What?

ARNIE: Bein' fast.
Move in fast. Move out fast.
I don't know.

MIKE: If you got problems with my mom, don't come crying on my shoulder!

ARNIE: I can handle my problems.
Now what should I tell your mother?!

MIKE: Tell her she's a slut.
(ARNIE *slaps him.*)
Tell her diggers in my bracket can't just walk off the job...
(*He laughs ironically.*)
...or they get fired.

(*Lights down.* ARNIE *leaves.*)

(*Sound and lights up on* HUMBERT *and* JOHNNY. *We hear an overlay of* "Georgia on My Mind" *on the radio.*)

JOHNNY: (*Singing along loudly*)
Georgia...Georgia....
(*Takes up his fiddle, ready to play, but doesn't*)
Nice state.
Think I'll add it to my collection.

(*Music fades. We hear distant thunder.*)

HUMBERT: Do you hear thunder?
Is that thunder?
Anybody up there?
Anybody home?
Hello.
Hello.
You're not going to tell me it was all a goddamned dream, are you?
A delusion, a dream, an hallucination,
and now here I am stranded alone.
God?
God.
(*He laughs.*)
So here I am, twilight.
Complete darkness out there

except for one little porch light lost in the hills.
Some poor bastard waiting out there
for someone, anyone, a knock on the door,
night closing in and what does that poor bastard have?
A light as big as a fingernail....
He should be up here
with a thousand lights burning overhead
and silver shining along the hills.
Maybe he wouldn't be so goddamn lonely.
Maybe, somehow, he'd see—what I know I'm finally
going to see— just how everything fades away up here
and is forgiven....
(Pause)
Johnny!
Hey, Johnnny!

JOHNNY: Yes?

HUMBERT: I can't build any higher.

JOHNNY: You sure?

HUMBERT: Yeh.

JOHNNY: Then I reckon it's done.
(Turns his music up)
Now if I could jest get this song down.

(Strains of "Georgia on my Mind." Fade out. Lights down.)

End of Scene Nine

Scene Ten

(HUMBERT *is high in the tower, out of sight. The house is altered. Most of the porch is gone and there are piles of bottles and cans in the yard. The vegetable stand is empty. The sign now reads, "TOWER PHOTOS $5.00, QUESTIONS ANSWERED."* JOHNNY, *dressed for early fall, is giving a talk. We see the flash of flashbulbs occasionally as he talks.)*

(CONNIE *approaches quietly and watches. She carries a red suitcase and a box; she wears a light sweater.*)

JOHNNY: Can't say as I ever heard of (*Mispronounces*) Zud Deutsche Zeitung but we got lots of papers comin' 'round, National Geographic come by last month. Yessir. We been workin' here fer a year and a half now. Piece of history in the making. Tower's six stories high. You can see clear over the Great Lakes goin' both ways. We used 246,000 bottles and 422,657 cans. Some was sent from as far away as Orlando, Florida. We got three thousand miles of wire and cable and used 478 storm winder frames. The bottom here (*He poses as he talks.*) spans forty feet and when she's finished, she'll be eight stories tall spannin' ten feet at the pinnacle. So do not neglect this opportunity, folks, to make your small contribution to history. Five bucks, if you please, more if you're willin'. Thank you, much obliged.
(HUMBERT *is climbing down. He looks wild, dressed only in shorts.* CONNIE *gasps and starts toward him.*)

JOHNNY: Sorry, Ma'am, no one's allowed on the premises
but if you'd like to make a small....
(CONNIE *puts the suitcase down.*)

CONNIE: Johnny!

JOHNNY: Oh, Missus, Missus, I'm sorry.

(HUMBERT *catches sight of her and is torn between wanting to run to her and away from her.*)

HUMBERT: Connie.

CONNIE: So you did use the house
like they said.

HUMBERT: Not your room.
Not the kitchen.
It's just as you left it.

(He brings a chair for her. He limps slightly.)
Here, make yourself at home.

CONNIE: Home.
Thank you.
(They look at each other. HUMBERT *is extremely self-conscious.)*
Aren't you cold?

HUMBERT: No.
Sun's hot up there....I....

CONNIE: Oh, Humbert, aren't you ashamed?

HUMBERT: I...look picturesque this way.
People would rather contribute...if they think....

CONNIE: If they think you're crazy.

HUMBERT: Yes.
(He shifts from foot to foot uncomfortably.)

CONNIE: What's the matter with your foot?

HUMBERT: I don't know.
Nothing much.

CONNIE: Let me see.

HUMBERT: Connie...I...
I need a bath.

CONNIE: Wouldn't be the first time.
Now let me see your foot.
(He puts his foot in her lap.)
Honestly, Humbert, you have to keep your nails trimmed.
They're cutting into your skin.
Get a chair and stop hopping around.
(She goes in the house and gets some clippers. He gets another chair. He is very sad.)

HUMBERT: So. How've you been?

CONNIE: Fine. Just fine and dandy.
Give me the other foot.

HUMBERT: Time passes.
(Pause)
Leaves are falling from the trees.

CONNIE: I know.

HUMBERT: It's another world up there, Con.

CONNIE: It must be.
Scampering around like a monkey in the treetops.
(Long pause)

HUMBERT: You can scamper up there too....
I built a little walkway for you,
winds right up to the top.
You can climb up
and stand there looking out over the trees.
It's wonderful, Con.
Vast!
Stretches of maple and birch and oak and sycamore,
cottonwood, spruce, balsam, white pine, poplar, walnut.

CONNIE: *(Laughs)*
You always did know their names!

HUMBERT: Names?! You want names?!
There's hickory and wild plum and ash trees and
dogwood and crabapple and chokeberries and weeping
willows by the streams.

CONNIE: *(Touches his face)*
I knew the birdcalls and you knew the trees.

HUMBERT: Connie, please come see it.

CONNIE: I don't need a tower to see.

HUMBERT: But you do.
How else can you see the entirety—the whole thing,
the dead trees standing with the living.
Dead and alive together

so straight they'll break your heart.
You only know which are dead and which alive when
spring comes again and the leaves open.
Even the dead trees have dignity.
A man falls down when he dies.

CONNIE: Why are you talking about death?
Don't you feel well?
Can't we talk about life or love or...aluminum siding...
(After a pause)
or us.

HUMBERT: I am talking about us.
I want you to believe me, Con. I'm not a madman,
I did it. I'm right. I've done something wonderful.
I recreated God's view of nature!
The only thing you can't see from there—is the future!

CONNIE: Then it's not God's view.
He can see the future.

HUMBERT: You don't believe me.
(Abruptly pulls his foot away and gets up)
Are you through?

CONNIE: Honestly, Humbert. Give a body half a chance!
We've got to get things back to normal!

HUMBERT: Normal? Why?
I like my nails long and my hair long and my beard grown!
I like what I'm doing and I like who I am.
(He gets very close to her and she backs away. He keeps approaching and she retreating.)

CONNIE: What's gotten into you?

HUMBERT: I like everything that's happening and everything that's happened. I am perfectly content.
Ha-ha-ha.

CONNIE: Johnny!
What's wrong?!

(JOHNNY *comes over.*)

HUMBERT: I am happy and you are happy. Blubba, blubba, blubba,
blubba grrr-rrrrrrrr.
(*Tries to scare her away. Then he plops into a chair and freezes, staring straight ahead.*)

CONNIE: Johnny, what is it?

JOHNNY: (*Passing his hand before* HUMBERT's *eyes*)
I don't rightly know,
Probably your visit just upset him a bit. He was fine before.

CONNIE: (*Sadly*)
I can't stop thinking about him. Can't eat. Can't hardly sleep. That's how he feels about the tower, isn't it? Great. I feel that way about him. He feels that way about the tower.

JOHNNY: You better sit down.
You look peaked, Missus.

CONNIE: I'm just tired. I haven't slept all night and I'm not quite myself.
(*Giddy*)
I'm somebody else
someplace else.
(*She lights her cigar.*)

JOHNNY: We got some cinnamon-walnut tea in the house.
You want some?

CONNIE: Sure.
(JOHNNY *exits.* CONNIE *paces, working herself up.*)
You know what the trouble is, Humbert?
It's not that you're crazy.

I can handle you crazy—
I did it before.
It's that you're proud.
You're so high and mighty
you think only you have dreams and only your
dreams matter.
But I'll tell you,
I have dreams too—
a lot of them
and not one
includes you.
(JOHNNY *enters.*)

JOHNNY: *(Giving her a cup)*
Honey's already there.

CONNIE: I've been wanting to come for so long.
(She jumps up.)
But I can't stay here. Lord!
Not one minute more!

(She takes the suitcase and runs. JOHNNY *opens the box.*
HUMBERT *comes over, very normal.)*

HUMBERT: Do you think she was glad to see me?

JOHNNY: You acted like a fool.

HUMBERT: I think she would have stayed.

JOHNNY: Not with you actin' like a fool.

HUMBERT: *(Long pause, anguished)*
What else could I do?
I have got to finish this tower
and I would give up everything
just to have her back with me.

(Lights out)

End of Scene Ten

Scene Eleven

(It is a bright Saturday in November. HUMBERT *is in the tower in shorts and a shirt.)*

*(*JOHNNY *is in an old jeans jacket, perhaps with a scarf. He is sitting, putting finishing touches on a sign that will read, "GRAND OPENING THE WONDERFUL TOWER, NOVEMBER 5, FREE ADMISSION. PHOTOS $8.00.)*

*(*HUMBERT *is throwing streamers of banners from different portions of the tower so he can string them across and decorate it for the opening. This is already partially done.)*

HUMBERT: *(Lets one loose)* Yahoo!
(Throws another and watches it)
This'll be a goddamn maypole!

(Car horn honks impatiently.)

JOHNNY: *(Crosses his arms on his chest)*
I ain't movin'.
(Car honks again.)
Tomorrow. Come back tomorrow. Can't you read?
(Waves them away impatiently)
You'd think those folks don't got eyes in their heads.
I put five big signs along the highway
sayin' the openin' is November 5th clear as day!

*(*HUMBERT *comes down, ties streamers in place.)*

HUMBERT: Now all we need are the people and we're through,
(Steps back to examine it)
finished.
One year, six months.

JOHNNY: And twenty-two days.

HUMBERT: *(Drawing it out)*
One year—six months—and—twenty-two—days.

(Goes to the bottom of the tower)
And what do you suppose they'll
really see up there?
(Sound of a car driving up)

JOHNNY: Uh-oh. We got company!

HUMBERT: *(Alarmed)*
Why the hell would these two be
coming here!

(MIKE and ARNIE walk in, dressed for fall. JOHNNY goes to meet them. HUMBERT keeps his back to them.)

JOHNNY: Howdy.

MIKE: Hi, Johnny.
(Makes a beeline for the house. Ignores HUMBERT.)

ARNIE: *(To JOHNNY)*
Hi there, pardner.
(Goes right to HUMBERT)
Hello, Humbert.

HUMBERT: *(Follows MIKE to the door)* Mikey?
(MIKE hesitates at the door. He is about to speak, doesn't, looks to ARNIE for support.)

ARNIE: Don't worry about it now, Son.
Just get the clothes.
(Puts his hand on HUMBERT's shoulder. HUMBERT moves away.)
Humbert.

HUMBERT: I guess you and him are pretty close?
(Laughs uneasily)
Yes, well. He needs a friend.
(Trying to make conversation)
Looks bigger...filled out around the shoulders....
More like a man I guess.
(Laughs again)

Time sure flies.
I haven't seen the boy in...ok....

ARNIE: In seven months....

JOHNNY: And fifteen days.

HUMBERT: Right.
It has been a while, hasn't it?
(Pause)
Uh...you want something?
Hey, Johnny, any Stroh's left?
(To ARNIE*)*
There isn't much.
I don't stock up with just the two of us here
and everything....
Maybe we still have a Coke, or some coffee....

ARNIE: I know I should have come by sooner.

HUMBERT: You know, I really don't feel like offering
you anything.
I mean, if the truth be known, I don't even want to talk
to you!
(He heads for the tower.)

ARNIE: You got to listen to me.

HUMBERT: Piss off, Arnie.

ARNIE: Look, this is hard enough....

HUMBERT: What do you know about hard?
You have your cushy little job,
and a warm little woman waiting for you at home.
We've got nothing to talk about...old buddy.
(Tries to go to tower)

ARNIE: We do, Humbert.
Connie's dead.
(Silence; no one moves.)
I said....

HUMBERT: I know what you said!

ARNIE: I...I found her this morning
in her chair by the window.
Her magazine had fallen on the floor...
the light was on....
I guess she couldn't sleep.
I did my best, you know?
But she'd lost her peace.
She'd just walk and walk and cry and walk.
I tried everything I could.
I'd hold her and rub her back
but she'd just smile and pat my hand, and get up again....

HUMBERT: Arnie....

ARNIE: She used to tell me she was halfway to heaven....
'Cause she turned forty, you know....
And I'd tease her. I'd say, "Halfway ain't nothin', darlin'....
Stick with me and I'll take you all the way...all the way...."
Wasn't much of a joke, was it?
(Tries to say something, stops, goes on)
I was never an exciting person to her, Humbert, but she was to me....
(Covers his face with his hands)

(HUMBERT starts toward ARNIE, perhaps to comfort him. MIKE comes out and HUMBERT retreats.)

MIKE: *(Has on a suit coat that is slightly small)*
The pants don't fit anymore.
Do you think the jacket's okay?

ARNIE: *(Trying to compose himself)* Sure.

MIKE: The pants don't fit anymore.

ARNIE: *(Puts his arm around MIKE)*
It's okay.
Jeans are dark.

MIKE: Mom wouldn't care.

ARNIE: It's just to show your love and respect.

HUMBERT: *(To* MIKE*)* Hey, kiddo.

MIKE: *(Makes a display of ignoring* HUMBERT*)*
There's some things of hers.
I'll need a box.
Johnny? Is there a box around here someplace?

JOHNNY: Eh?

HUMBERT: You can't take her things.

MIKE: Johnny?

(JOHNNY *is undecided. Takes his cue from* HUMBERT *and stays back.)*

HUMBERT: Leave her things.

MIKE: Why?
So you can rip them up?

HUMBERT: She left them here. They are mine.
(MIKE *doesn't respond and looks around for a box.*
HUMBERT *follows him.)*

MIKE: There must be a box or a bag or something.
(JOHNNY *rummages around with him.)*

HUMBERT: If she wanted them, she would have taken them with her. She took everything else—pots, pans, sewing kit, nightgowns, pictures, sheets...even her goddamn garden trowel.

MIKE: Don't you curse when you mention her!

HUMBERT: I'll curse if I damn well please!
This is my house, buddy boy, and she left!
She walked out!
(MIKE *tries to avoid him, but* HUMBERT *follows.)*
She could have waited, tried to understand!
How long did it take to do this—two years? Not even

two years!
What's two years in a lifetime? There were years I didn't understand her either! Did I leave?! Did I walk out?!
She could have had a fling with Arnie here, a little thing on the side, if she was so pissed off.
She didn't have to go and leave me!

MIKE: I did too, remember?

ARNIE: Don't do this now.

HUMBERT: Stay out of this!

ARNIE: *(Puts his hand on* HUMBERT's *shoulder, trying to calm him and seek comfort)*
She's dead, Humbert.

HUMBERT: *(Strikes out blindly at him)*
Keep your hands off me!
(ARNIE *stumbles back.* MIKE *grabs* HUMBERT *and throws him to the ground and stands over him. The three should be utterly surprised at this turn of events.)*

MIKE: Leave him alone!
(Stands, straddling him)
You freak!

ARNIE: *(Pulls him off toward the house)*
It's okay, kid. It's okay.
Back off....
That's it...back off.

(ARNIE *guides* MIKE *into the house.* HUMBERT *sits up, dazed.* JOHNNY *approaches.)*

JOHNNY: Things got a little out of hand.
*(*HUMBERT *stands up unsteadily.)*
Maybe you should sit back down fer a minute here.

HUMBERT: I'm all right.
(He sits down anyway.)

JOHNNY: *(Hesitantly)* I'm sorry about the missus.

HUMBERT: She died thinking I was a fool.

JOHNNY: Guess she did.

HUMBERT: I robbed her of her home and her peace and she died knowing I was a fool.
(Goes to the tower)
Pile of junk.
God's view, my ass!
God flicked his little finger and Connie died.
That's God, life and death—
not junk!
(He kicks it.)
Shit.
(He cries quietly.)

JOHNNY: I'm really sorry.
Wish I could help.

HUMBERT: *(Stares at him)*
Do you believe in everlasting life, Johnny?

JOHNNY: Yep.

HUMBERT: Are you born that way
or can you learn it?

JOHNNY: I reckon you can't learn it like a fact.
But if you see things right, you can understand it.

HUMBERT: I want to find Connie again.
(He jumps up suddenly, filled with energy, starts looking for his clothes.)
Do you got a comb, Johnny, I better neaten up!
(JOHNNY hands it to him.)
Thanks.
(Starts getting dressed as he talks, with growing excitement)
You said living things come back according to their nature, didn't you?

JOHNNY: Yep.

HUMBERT: If they lived in woods, it's woods....
(Pause, considering)
Connie loves woods.
But she likes neighbors. So she wouldn't be way out in the woods.
She likes a couple shops too where everyone knows her and she can smoke those damn cigars....
There'd have to be a house...a little one.
She never did like housework....
But there'd have to be a big stove....
(Starts getting dressed, adding shoes, shirt, and so on)
And there'd be a garden with melon vines and tomato plants,
wildflowers...nothing too tame, you know....
Oh! We should look for one of those tall, white Anglican churches with stained glass and bells. The works!
She likes to pray in style!
(Checks his appearance—hair, pants, shirt)
Do you think I can find her with that description?

JOHNNY: Maybe so. Lots of places like that northwest of here.
(Smiles broadly)
Fact is, the other day I thought I saw a two-peaked mountain northwest of here.
Clouds come up and covered it, but it sure looked familiar. Like to go see it. How about you?
I got five bucks. What you got?

HUMBERT: Three, three-fifty.
(Checking his pockets)
I don't know.

JOHNNY: We don't need much.

HUMBERT: Hardly a thing.

JOHNNY: So?

HUMBERT: I'm ready.
(JOHNNY *gets his fiddle and checks his equipment and hands* HUMBERT *a fistful of cigars.*)
Guess I almost forgot my peace offering!
(*He scribbles something on a piece of paper and tacks it onto the tower. They start off.*)
Say, can you play the fiddle while we're walking?

JOHNNY: Sure can.
(*Tunes it*)

HUMBERT: Do you know....
(*Pauses to consider*)
"Amazing Grace"?

(*They walk off.* JOHNNY *plays* "Amazing Grace." *The yard is empty for a moment.* ARNIE *comes out.*)

ARNIE: Humbert?
(*Calling*)
Humbert!
(*He doesn't see anybody. It's very still. The note catches his eye. He goes to it and reads it.* MIKE *comes out, some of* CONNIE's *clothes draped over his arm.*)

MIKE: We can just carry it.

ARNIE: (*Takes the note off the tower*)
You got a note here, Son.
(*Hands him the note*)

MIKE: What?!
(*Snatches it, reads it*)
Can you believe this?!
"Dear Mike,
I went to find your Mom.
In the meantime, everything I have is yours.
Signed
Humbert Lavoignet
November 4, [current year]."
(*Crumples the note*)

Dad! Dad!
(Starts searching frantically)

ARNIE: You know how he's been.

MIKE: He's not going to get away with this!
I'll find him!

ARNIE: We can take the van.

MIKE: *(Goes to the tower and clambers up)*
I'll spot him from here.
Catch him in his own trap!
(Climbs)
Jerk! Coward!
Thinks you can run away
every time there's trouble!
What's the matter with him?
Why does he do it? Disappear!
Every fucking time—
something's wrong—up the tower!
Got a problem?—Up the tower.
Need some help—up the tower. Need anything—up the damn tower!

ARNIE: Can you see him?

MIKE: Nope.
(Stops and looks)

ARNIE: Can't have gone far.
Probably behind a tree or something.

MIKE: *(Cups his hands around his mouth and yells)*
Daaad?
(Quieter)
Dad?
(Falls silent)
I can't see him, Arnie, he's disappeared.

ARNIE: Hold on a minute.

MIKE: *(Climbs higher)* Arnie?

ARNIE: Be patient.

MIKE: I can see for miles up here...miles and miles....
(Turns around in all directions)
Miles and miles....
(He strains to locate him.)
He's gone.

ARNIE: Don't worry, kid, you'll find him.

MIKE: I don't know.
(Silence between them. We hear wind.)

ARNIE: Maybe it's time for you to come down now.

MIKE: *(Something catches his eye)*
Look at the damn highway crew struttin' their stuff.
They think they're really hot shit—
look like little roosters to me.
Hey, guys. Heyyyyy.

(Perhaps we see JOHNNY *and* HUMBERT *in silhouette. Perhaps we only hear a faint strain of "Amazing Grace," as if brought by the wind.)*

ARNIE: Mike,
we should go.

MIKE: You'd think I could see him from here.
The land goes on forever.

(Lights slowly dim until MIKE *is isolated on the tower. The wind is blowing. We hear it.* MIKE *raises his collar, peers into the growing darkness. We hear "Will the Circle Be Unbroken.")*

ARNIE: Mike.

MIKE: There's a huge stretch of trees, Arnie.
You should see 'em.
Must be a million. One after another after another sooo straight....
(His voice trails off.)
Do you know what kind of trees those are?

Lived around here all my life,
but I never learned their names.

(Music up. Lights down. Blackout.)

End of Play

www.ingramcontent.com/pod-product-compliance
Lightning Source LLC
Chambersburg PA
CBHW060217050426
42446CB00013B/3093